YOUR KNOWLEDGE HA

Ninad Gondhalekar

Verilog Design of a Pedestrian Crossing

Verilog Programming

GRIN Publishing

Bibliographic information published by the German National Library:

The German National Library lists this publication in the National Bibliography; detailed bibliographic data are available on the Internet at http://dnb.dnb.de .

Imprint:

Copyright © 2013 GRIN Verlag GmbH
Print and binding: Books on Demand GmbH, Norderstedt Germany
ISBN: 978-3-656-84502-7

This book at GRIN:

http://www.grin.com/en/e-book/284210/verilog-design-of-a-pedestrian-crossing

GRIN - Your knowledge has value

Since its foundation in 1998, GRIN has specialized in publishing academic texts by students, college teachers and other academics as e-book and printed book. The website www.grin.com is an ideal platform for presenting term papers, final papers, scientific essays, dissertations and specialist books.

Visit us on the internet:

http://www.grin.com/

http://www.facebook.com/grincom

http://www.twitter.com/grin_com

Beng. Electrical and Electronic Engineering
(Hons.)

EN0628 Digital System Design and Implementation
(2013)

Report – 2

Verilog Design of a Pedestrian Crossing

Controller

Name – Ninad Gondhalekar

Date of Submission – 2/05/2013

Contents

Introduction

This laboratory results shows the Verilog hardware design language (HDL) and Finite State Machine to control a pedestrian crossing controller and its modification. In session – 1, simple Verilog program is simulated and then tested on Coolrunner – II board. In this session the controller three outside world input which are Clock (CLK), Reset (RESET), Pedestrian (PED) and three output which are Red light (RED), Amber light (AMBER), Green light (GREEN).

In session – 2, some modifications are done on Verilog program used in session – 1 and then again simulated and tested on Coolrunner – II board. In this session the controller 7 segment displays is used to see changes in pelstate, while running modified Verilog program on Coolrunner – II board and Carsensor outside world input has been introduced in modified Verilog program. In this modified Verilog program, number of pelstate has been increased.

This laboratory session provides a good opportunity to learn Xilinx ISE Design Suit software and introduce to Coolrunner – II board.

Session - I

Block diagram of finite state machine of pelican crossing controller used in session – I is shown in figure 1. There are three inputs are given by outside world to FSM controller (pelcont), which is pedestrian, clock and reset. The controller has three outputs red, amber and green light. There is no direct connection between output and input. Two counters (FRTIMER and TIMER) are used to create timer and flash and are fed with clock signal. The TIMER module is used to count long, medium and short time and FRTIMER is used to flash amber light. The clock frequency is 10 KHz.

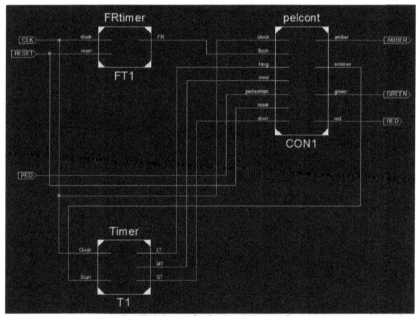

Fig 1: Block diagram of pedestrian crossing controller.

Verilog modules and 'ucf' file for session – I
Top – level description

```
//top-level verilog description of pedestrian crossing system
module pelican(input CLK, PED, RESET,
                output AMBER, GREEN, RED);

    wire ET;
    wire FL;
    wire LT;
    wire MT;
    wire ST;
```

4

```
pelcont CON1 (.clock(CLK),
        .flash(FL),
        .long(LT),
        .med(MT),
        .pedestrian(PED),
        .reset(RESET),
        .short(ST),
        .amber(AMBER),
        .entimer(ET),
        .green(GREEN),
        .red(RED));
FRtimer FT1 (.clock(CLK),
        .reset(RESET),
        .FR(FL));
Timer T1 (.Clock(CLK),
        .Start(ET),
        .LT(LT),
        .MT(MT),
        .ST(ST));
endmodule
```

Top level description shows the connection of module pelcont (CON1), FRtimer (FT1), Timer (T1) with each other.

Test_Pelican module

```
`timescale 1 us/1 us

module test_pelican;

  reg CLK;
  reg PED;
  reg RESET;

  wire AMBER;
  wire GREEN;
  wire RED;

  initial      // 10kHz Clock process for CLK
  begin
    CLK = 1'b0; // CLK = 1
    forever
    #50 CLK = ~CLK; // CLK toggles every 50 us
  end

  pelican UUT (
    .CLK(CLK),
    .PED(PED),
    .RESET(RESET),
    .AMBER(AMBER),
    .GREEN(GREEN),
    .RED(RED));

  initial begin

                PED = 1'b0;   //PED =1
                RESET = 1'b1; // reset = 1

                //wait 10 clocks
  repeat (10) @(negedge CLK);
  RESET = 1'b0;          // reset = 0
```

```
                    //wait 40 seconds, then pulse PED
        repeat (400000) @(negedge CLK);
        PED = 1'b1;    // ped = 1

        repeat (100) @(negedge CLK);
        PED = 1'b0;    // ped = 0

                    //wait 50 seconds
                    repeat (500000) @(negedge CLK);

                    $stop;

    end
endmodule
```

Test_pelican module is used for simulation. It provides the clock for whole system for simulation process.

FSM pelcont module

```
//FSM for pelican crossing system
module pelcont(input clock, reset, pedestrian, short, med, long, flash,
          output red, amber, green, entimer);

//state assignments
localparam s0 = 3'b000, s1=3'b001, s2=3'b010, s3=3'b011,
         s4=3'b100, s5=3'b101, s6=3'b110;
                    //pelstate register is 3 bit register as 6 states are used (2^3 = 8)
reg [2:0] pelstate;    // pelstate should be register to store its current state value
                    //state register and next state logic
always @(posedge clock or posedge reset)        // at positive / rising edge of clock or reset input
begin
        if (reset)                  // if reset =1, pelstate = 0
                pelstate <= s0;
        else                        // if reset =0
                case (pelstate)
                    s0 : pelstate <= s1;            // pelstate = s1 (non-blocking)
                    s1 : pelstate <= (long)? s2 : s1; //if long =1, pelstate =s2 else  pelstate = s1
                    s2 : pelstate <= s3;            // pelstate =s3
                    s3 : pelstate <= (med)? s5 : ((flash)? s4 : s3); // if med = 1, pelstate = s5 else s4 if flash
                                                    //   =1 or pelstate = s3 if flash =0
                    s4 : pelstate <= (med)? s5 : ((flash)? s3 : s4); // if med = 1, pelstate = s5 else s3 if flash
                                                    //   =1 or pelstate = s4 if flash =0
                    s5 : pelstate <= (pedestrian)? s6 : s5;     // if pedestrian =1, pelstate = s6 else pelstate = s5
                    s6 : pelstate <= (short)? s0 : s6;      // if short = 1, pelstate = s0 else pelstate = s6
                default : pelstate <= 3'bx;            // default (don't care)
                    endcase
end

//state machine Moore o/p logic
//timer is on for pelstate 1,  3, 4 and 6
assign entimer = pelstate==s1||pelstate==s3||pelstate==s4||pelstate==s6;

//traffic lights assume active low LEDs
assign red = ~(pelstate==s1||pelstate==s0);  // red light is on for pelstate 1 and 0
assign amber = ~(pelstate==s2||pelstate==s3||pelstate==s6); // amber light is on for pelstate 2, 3 and 6
assign green= ~(pelstate==s5);  // green light is on for pelstate 5

endmodule
```

FRtimer module

```
module FRtimer(input clock, reset, output FR);

//time delay for flash (based on 10kHz clock)
parameter frtime=5000;

reg [12:0] q;  // q must be be register to store it current value and its 13 bits  (2^13 = 8192)

always @(posedge clock)   // at positive/ rising edge of clock
begin
        if (reset||q==frtime)  // if reset or q = frtime or both
                q <= 0;         // q = 0 (non-blocking)
        else
                q <= q + 1;     // if reset =0 and q is not equal to frtime then increase q by 1
end

assign FR = (q==frtime);   // FR output goes high if q is equal to frtime

endmodule
```

Timer module

```
module Timer(input Clock, Start, output ST, MT, LT);

//time delay values for light sequence
//based on 10kHz clock
parameter stime=50000, mtime=80000, ltime=200000;

reg [17:0] q;  // q must be register to store its current value  and is 18 bits (2^18 = 262144)

always @(posedge Clock) // at positive/ rising edge of clock
begin
        if (!Start||(q==ltime)) // if start =0 or q = 200000 or both are true
                q <= 0;         // q = 0 (non-blocking)
        else                    // if start=1 and q is not equal to 200000
                q <= q + 1;     // increase q by 1
end

//decode counter outputs for delay pulses
assign ST = (q==stime);    // ST = 1 if q = 50000
assign MT = (q==mtime);    // MT =1 if q = 80000
assign LT = (q==ltime);    // LT = 1 if q = 200000

endmodule
```

Pelicon ucf file

```
#PACE: Start of Constraints generated by PACE
#PACE: Start of PACE I/O Pin Assignments
NET "AMBER"  LOC = "P87" ;
NET "CLK"  LOC = "P38" ;
NET "GREEN"  LOC = "P86" ;
NET "PED"  LOC = "P60" ;
NET "RED"  LOC = "P131" ;
NET "RESET"  LOC = "P61" ;
#PACE: Start of PACE Area Constraints
#PACE: Start of PACE Prohibit Constraints
#PACE: End of Constraints generated by PACE
```

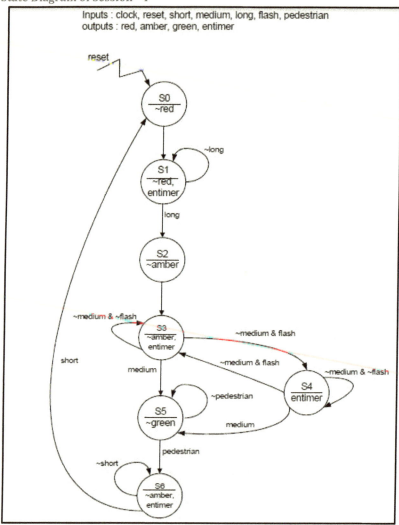

Fig 2: Block Diagram for Session – I

Simulation for Session – I

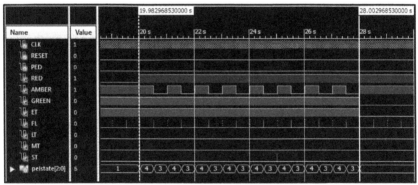

Fig 3: Simulation showing pelstate 0,1 and 2

(timing 20 sec, lights active low, state 0 and 2 state for only one clock cycle (i.e. 0.1ms) ET goes low in state2 and become high in state3, when program goes in state 3 but at same time flash goes high so according to state diagram program goes in state 4 and as FL goes low program goes in state 3. Change in ST,MT and LT affects output only if ET is high . In other words wherever timer is required, program keep ET high.)

Fig 4: Simulation showing pelstate 3 and 4

(comment on lights timing 8 sec MT goes high for 1 clock cycle, ET goes low when program moves in state 5 because only when PED goes high, program goes in state 6)

9

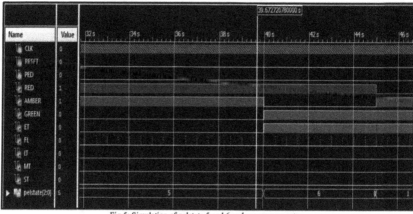

Fig 5: Simulation of pelstate 5 and 6 and program repeats.

(comment on lights, explain with help of state diagram

Explain all signals with help of Verilog language.)

CPLD Fitting Report for Session – I

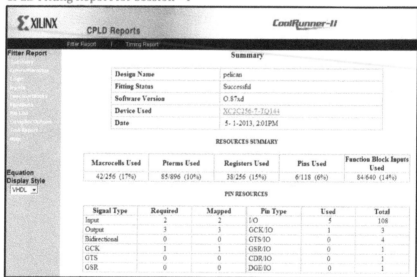

XILINX
CPLD Reports

CoolRunner-II

Fitter Report | Timing Report

Fitter Report

Summary

Design Name	pelican
Fitting Status	Successful
Software Version	0.87xd
Device Used	XC2C256-7-TQ144
Date	5- 1-2013, 2:01PM

RESOURCES SUMMARY

Macrocells Used	Pterms Used	Registers Used	Pins Used	Function Block Inputs Used
42/256 (17%)	85/896 (10%)	38/256 (15%)	6/118 (6%)	84/640 (14%)

Equation Display Style
VHDL

PIN RESOURCES

Signal Type	Required	Mapped	Pin Type	Used	Total
Input	2	2	I/O	5	108
Output	3	3	GCK/IO	1	3
Bidirectional	0	0	GTS/IO	0	4
GCK	1	1	GSR/IO	0	1
GTS	0	0	CDR/IO	0	1
GSR	0	0	DGE/IO	0	1

Fig 6: CPLD Fitting Report for Session – I

10

Working of Program on Coolrunner – II

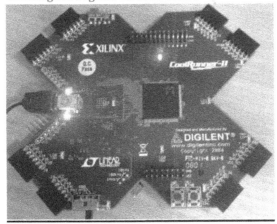

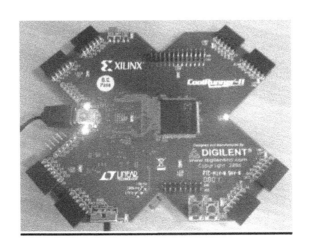

Session - II

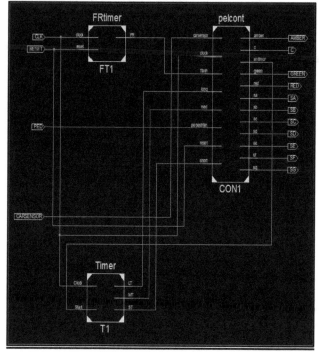

Fig 7: Block Diagram of Session – II

Block diagram of modified finite state machine of pelican crossing controller used in session – II is shown in Fig 7. There are four inputs are given by outside world to FSM controller (pelcont), which is car sensor, pedestrian, clock and reset. The controller has eleven outputs 8 outputs for seven segment display, red, amber and green light. There is no direct connection between output and input. Two counters (FRTIMER and TIMER) are used to create timer and flash and are fed with clock signal same as session - I. The TIMER module is used to count long, medium and short time and FRTIMER is used to flash amber light. The clock frequency is 10 KHz.

State Diagram for Session – II

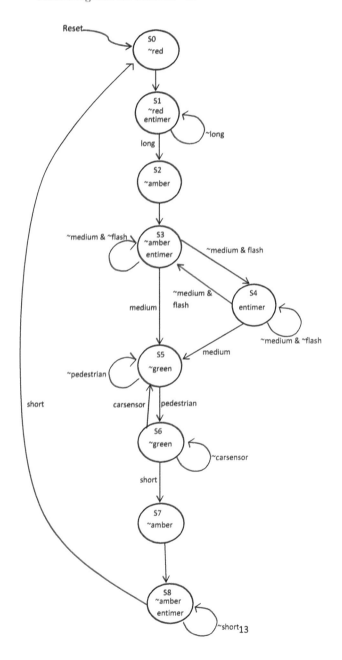

Verilog modules and 'ucf' file for session – II

Top Level Description

```
//top-level verilog description of pedestrian crossing system
module pelican(input CLK, PED, RESET, CARSENSOR,
                output AMBER, GREEN, RED,
                SA, SB, SC, SD, SE, SF, SG);

    wire ET;
    wire FL;
    wire LT;
    wire MT;
    wire ST;

    pelcont CON1 (.clock(CLK),
            .flash(FL),
            .long(LT),
            .med(MT),
            .pedestrian(PED),
            .reset(RESET),
            .short(ST),
            .carsensor(CARSENSOR),
            .amber(AMBER),
            .entimer(ET),
            .green(GREEN),
            .red(RED),
            .sa(SA),
            .sb(SB),
            .sc(SC),
            .sd(SD),
            .se(SE),
            .sf(SF),
            .sg(SG));
    FRtimer FT1 (.clock(CLK),
            .reset(RESET),
            .FR(FL));

    Timer T1 (.Clock(CLK),
            .Start(ET),
            .LT(LT),
            .MT(MT),
            .ST(ST));

endmodule
```

Top level description shows the connection of module pelcont (CON1), FRtimer (FT1), Timer (T1) with each other.

Test_pelican module

```
`timescale 1 us/1 us

module test_pelican;

    reg CLK;
    reg PED;
    reg RESET;
    reg CARSENSOR;

    wire AMBER;
```

14

```
wire GREEN;
wire RED;
wire SA, SB, SC, SD, SE, SF, SG;

initial    // 10kHz Clock process for CLK
begin
  CLK = 1'b0;
  forever
                        #50 CLK = ~CLK;
end

pelican UUT (
                .CLK(CLK),
                .PED(PED),
                .RESET(RESET),
                .CARSENSOR(CARSENSOR),
                .AMBER(AMBER),
                .GREEN(GREEN),
                .RED(RED),
                .SA(SA),
                .SB(SB),
                .SC(SC),
                .SD(SD),
                .SE(SE),
                .SF(SF),
                .SG(SG));

initial begin

                PED = 1'b0;
                CARSENSOR = 1'b0;
                RESET = 1'b1;

  //wait 10 clocks
  repeat (10) @(negedge CLK);
  RESET = 1'b0;

                //wait 40 seconds, then pulse PED
  repeat (400000) @(negedge CLK);
  PED = 1'b1;

  repeat (10000) @(negedge CLK);
  PED = 1'b0;

                repeat (20000) @(negedge CLK);
                CARSENSOR = 1'b1;            // carsensor =1

                repeat (10000) @(negedge CLK);
                CARSENSOR = 1'b0;            //carsensor =0

                //wait 50 seconds
                repeat (500000) @(negedge CLK);

                $stop;
  end
endmodule
```

FSM pelicont module

```
//FSM for pelican crossing system
module pelcont (input clock, reset, pedestrian, short, med, long,
```

15

```verilog
                    flash, carsensor,
                output red, amber, green, entimer,
                    sa, sb, sc, sd, se, sf, sg,);

//state assignments
localparam s0 = 4'b0000, s1=4'b0001, s2=4'b0010, s3=4'b0011,
                                s4=4'b0100, s5=4'b0101, s6=4'b0110,
                                s7=4'b0111, s8=4'b1000;

reg [3:0] pelstate; //state register

//state register and next state logic
always @(posedge clock or posedge reset)
begin
        if (reset)
                pelstate <= s0;
        else
                case (pelstate)
                        s0 : pelstate <= s1;
                        s1 : pelstate <= (long)? s2 : s1;
                        s2 : pelstate <= s3;
                        s3 : pelstate <= (med)? s5 : ((flash)? s4 : s3);
                        s4 : pelstate <= (med)? s5 : ((flash)? s3 : s4);
                        s5 : pelstate <= (pedestrian)? s6 : s5;
                        s6 : pelstate <= (short)? s7 : ((carsensor)? s5 : s6);
                        s7 : pelstate <= s8;
                        s8 : pelstate <= (short)? s0 : s8;
                    default : pelstate <= 4'bx;
                endcase
end

//state machine Moore o/p logic
//timer enable
assign entimer = pelstate==s1||pelstate==s3||pelstate==s4||pelstate==s6||pelstate==s8;

//traffic lights assume active low LEDs
assign red = ~(pelstate==s1||pelstate==s0);
assign amber = ~(pelstate==s2||pelstate==s3||pelstate==s7||pelstate==s8);
assign green= ~(pelstate==s5||pelstate==s6);

// 7-segment display (common anode)
assign sa = ~(pelstate==s1||pelstate==s4);   //sa =0 when pelstate =s1 , s4
assign sb = ~(pelstate==s5||pelstate==s6);  // sb =0 when pelstate = s5,s6
assign sc = ~(pelstate==s2);            // sc = 0 when pelstate = s2
assign sd = ~(pelstate==s1||pelstate==s4||pelstate==s7); //sd=0 when pelstate = s1, s4, s7
assign se = ~(pelstate==s1||pelstate==s3||pelstate==s4 ||pelstate==s5||pelstate==s7); // se =0 when pelstate=
                                                                //s1, s3,s4, s5, s7
assign sf = ~(pelstate==s1||pelstate==s2
         ||pelstate==s3||pelstate==s7); // sf = 0 when pelstate =s1,s2,s3,s7
assign sg = ~(pelstate==s0||pelstate==s1||pelstate==s7); // sg = 0 when pelstate =s0,s1,s7

endmodule
```

FRtimer module

```verilog
module FRtimer(input clock, reset, output FR);

//time delay for flash (based on 10kHz clock)
```

```
parameter frtime=5000;

reg [12:0] q;  // q must be be register to store it current value and its 13 bits (2^13 = 8192)

always @(posedge clock)  // at positive/ rising edge of clock
begin
        if (reset||q==frtime)  // if reset or q = frtime or both
                q <= 0;        // q = 0 (non-blocking)
        else
                q <= q + 1;    // if reset =0 and q is not equal to frtime then increase q by 1
end

assign FR = (q==frtime);   // FR output goes high if q is equal to frtime

endmodule
```

Timer Module

```
module Timer(input Clock, Start, output ST, MT, LT);

//time delay values for light sequence
//based on 10kHz clock
parameter stime=50000, mtime=80000, ltime=200000;

reg [17:0] q;  // q must be register to store its current value  and is 18 bits (2^18 = 262144)

always @(posedge Clock) // at positive/ rising edge of clock
begin
        if (!Start||(q==ltime)) // if start =0 or q = 200000 or both are true
                q <= 0;         // q = 0 (non-blocking)
        else                    // if start=1 and q is not equal to 200000
                q <= q + 1;     // increase q by 1
end

//decode counter outputs for delay pulses
assign ST = (q==stime);   // ST = 1 if q = 50000
assign MT = (q==mtime);   // MT =1 if q = 80000
assign LT = (q==ltime);   // LT = 1 if q = 200000

endmodule
```

Pelicon ucf file

```
#PACE: Start of Constraints generated by PACE
#PACE: Start of PACE I/O Pin Assignments
NET "RED"  LOC = "P131" ;
NET "AMBER"  LOC = "P87" ;
NET "GREEN"  LOC = "P86" ;
NET "CLK"  LOC = "P38" ;
NET "PED"  LOC = "P60" ;
NET "CARSENSOR" LOC = "P82" ;
NET "RESET"  LOC = "P61" ;
NET "SA" LOC = "P43";
NET "SB" LOC = "P42";
NET "SC" LOC = "P41";
NET "SD" LOC = "P40";
NET "SE" LOC = "P39";
NET "SF" LOC = "P35";
NET "SG" LOC = "P34";
NET "C" LOC = "P33";
#PACE: Start of PACE Area Constraints
#PACE: Start of PACE Prohibit Constraints
```

Simulation for Session - II

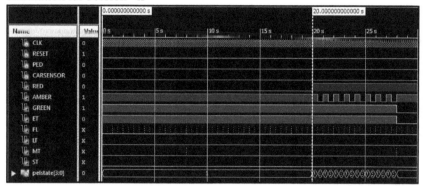

Fig 8: Simulation showing pelstate 0, 1 and 2

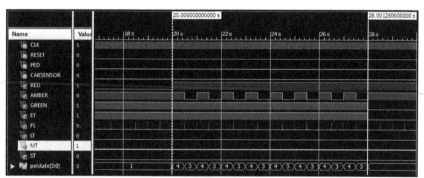

Fig 9: Simulation showing pelstate 3 and 4

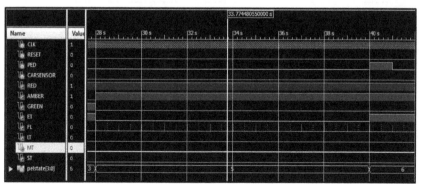

Fig 10: Simulation showing pelstate 5 and 6

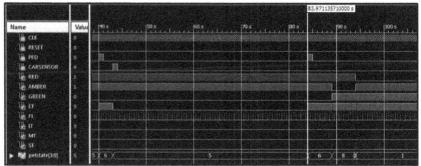

Fig 11: Simulation showing pelstate 5, 6, 7 and 8 and then repeatation

Simulation of session –II is same as session – I till pelstate 4, only state 5 and 6 state are different from session – I due to car sensor input and pelstate 8 is added in session – II. After entering in pelstate 5, program stays in state 5 till pedestrian button (PED) is pressed. When program stays in pelstate 5, green light is on and red and amber light is off (active low) as can be seen in Fig 11 green is low and red and amber is high. When program goes in pelstate 6 enable-timer (ET) is on to start timer for 5 sec approx. but if carsensor goes high when program is in pelstate 6, program again goes in pelstate 5 and disable enable-timer (ET=0) and waits for pedestrian button (PED) to go high, as shown in Fig 11. If carsensor doesn't goes high when program is pelstate 6, program goes in pelstate 8 when (ST =1) and wait for ST to go high again. When ST goes high, program goes back in pelstate 0. In Fig 11 Spike can be seen in ST input in between pelstate 6 and 8; pelstate 8 and 0.

19

CPLD Fitting Report for Session – II

Fig 11: CPLD Fitting Report for Session – II

Working of Program on Coolrunner – II

Conclusion

Both Sessions were completed in lab with simulations and testing both programs on Coolrunner – II CPLD board. The modified program used 52 /256 macrocells (21%), 103/896 Pterms (12%), 40/256 registers (16%), 15/118 Pins (13%) and 97/640 function block Inputs (16%). The original program used 42/256 Macrocells (17%), 85/896 Pterms (10%), 38/256 registers (15%), 6/118 Pins (6%) and 84/640 function block Inputs (14%). That means modified program only used 4% macrocells, 2%Pterms, 1% registers, 6% pins and 2 % function block inputs more compared to macrocells used by original program.

The Verilog hardware language is very convenient to design a system and to modify it. It's easy to add inputs or outputwithout modifying much codes. Implementation of system on Xilinx board is very easy and it's convenient to design other systems using Xilinx's FPGA.

20